THE CREATIVE ART OF

Dried Flowers

THE CREATIVE ART OF

Dried Flowers

Sarah Waterkeyn

Longmeadow Press

The Creative Art of Dried Flowers

This 1989 edition published by
Longmeadow Press,
201 High Ridge Road,
Stamford, CT 06904.

ISBN 0-681-40724-7

© Salamander Books Ltd. 1988
52 Bedford Row,
London WC1R 4LR,
United Kingdom.

CREDITS

Floral designs by: Sarah Waterkeyn and John Lewis

Editor-in-chief: Jilly Glassborow

Editor: Coral Walker

Designer: Barry Savage

Photographer: Steve Tanner

Typeset by: The Old Mill, London

Color separation by: Fotographics Ltd, London – Hong Kong

Printed in Italy

—————CONTENTS—————

INTRODUCTION

Today, dried flower arranging is a fashionable and exciting pastime. It is no longer associated with a few dark and dusty plants hidden away in a corner, but with displays as packed with colour and variety as any fresh flower arrangement. And the displays are there to be enjoyed for years rather than merely days.

With detailed step-by-step instructions, this book will show you how to create an exciting array of imaginative designs — garlands, wreaths, mobiles, pomanders, pot-pourri, centrepieces and many more. There is also essential information on what to buy, how to dry your own flowers, the equipment you will need, plus the various techniques employed. To help you identify the plants used throughout the book there is also a colour plate on pages 18/19 showing you twenty of the more common ones.

In most cases, flowers have been given their common names — except in those instances where the Latin is more often used. But as the naming of flowers tends to vary from one florist to another — some using common names, others Latin — the scientific names of plants have also been given at the back of the book.

DRIED FLOWERS

In recent years the popularity of dried flowers has soared as the variety and availability of plant material has increased one-hundred-fold. Whereas twenty years ago choice was restricted to a few common flowers and grasses, such as pampas grass, helichrysum (strawflowers or everlasting) and limonium (statice and sea lavender), today a host of specialist shops are bursting with exciting and colourful flowers from all over the world — plants such as proteas, dryandras and leucodendrons.

BUYING DRIED FLOWERS

When buying dried flowers, the wide range of plants now available may at first seem confusing. The beginner might be well advised to start by purchasing mixed bunches which can usually be bought in large departmental stores, gift shops and some fresh flower shops. But for real variety, it is best to buy individual bunches from a specialist shop. Often, only three or four varieties are all you need to create a colourful and imaginative display.

Decide what colours you want first, either choosing complementary colours such as yellows and oranges, reds and pinks, blues and purples or picking strikingly contrasting colours — yellows and purples, reds and blues, pinks and oranges. Think also about tonal contrast in your arrangement: white and yellow add welcome highlights to dark displays; dark browns or greens give depth to bright arrangements.

Shape and texture are also very important when planning a display; unusual shapes and contrasting textures add interest and can prevent an arrangement from looking uninspired. The illustration opposite shows some of the more unusual things you can add to your designs, including nuts, cones, fungi, twigs, spices and coral. Ribbons and fabric can also add colour and interest. So when gathering materials for your arrangements, try looking further than your local florist.

GROWING YOUR OWN

Growing your own flowers is by far the cheapest way of pursuing this hobby and has the advantage of providing you with colour in the garden as well as inside the home. Plants should be picked on a dry day just before the flowers are fully open, and preferably in the middle of the day when the sap is rising. If the flowers you pick are wet from rain or dew, before you preserve them, gently shake them and leave

A wide range of materials can be used to add interest to arrangements. Shown below are: 1) pot-pourri; 2) lotus seedheads; 3) repens rosette; 4) platyspernum cones; 5) Leucodendron plumosum; 6) walnuts; 7) coral; 8) sponge mushroom; 9) lagenaria fruit; 10) gourds; 11) artificial berries; 12) willow branch; 13) tallscreen; 14) lomius; 15) cinnamon sticks; 16) Spanish root; 17) cones.

them standing in some shallow water until the petals are dry.

One of the easiest methods of drying flowers is to hang them upside down in a warm, dark, airy place; this helps to preserve the flowers' natural colour. Not all plants are suitable for drying this way though — others are better preserved using desiccants or glycerine. Drying methods are discussed in more detail on overleaf.

To avoid leaving large bare patches in your garden after you have gathered the flowers, intersperse the flowers amongst other plants when planting so that their loss is not so noticeable later on. Suitable plants to grow for drying include everlastings such as helichrysums (strawflowers), helipterums (sunrays), xeranthemums and eryngium (sea holly), plus heathers, limonium, larkspur, golden rod, yarrow, lavender, lady's mantle, alliums and poppies. Dried roses are beautiful, but multi-petalled varieties are more suitable for preserving than single-petalled ones.

Also consider growing grasses, ferns and bracken for contrast in your arrangements. Foliage is also important: beech, holly, ivy, bay, hornbeam, box and lime are all good for preserving.

If you don't have a garden, pot plants can be a source of material. And keep an eye open on country walks; gather cones, bark, nuts and interesting shaped twigs from woodlands; wild flowers from meadows and hedgerows. Try experimenting with as many plants as you can to see if they are suitable for drying.

DRYING METHODS

There are a number of different ways of drying flowers and foliage and on page 126 you will find a table listing various plants and their methods of preservation. One of the easiest methods is air drying. A number of flowers (particularly the everlastings) can simply be left hanging upside down to dry in a warm, dark, airy place such as an airing cupboard, attic, loft or garage. It is important that the flowers are not put in direct sunlight as this will cause their colours to fade. Bind the flowers together into bunches before hanging them. Rubber bands are best for this purpose as the stems will shrink as they dry. Alternatively, use raffia, pipe cleaners or gardeners' string, being sure to tighten it around the stems regularly.

Suspend the flowers from a pole or some rope and leave them till they are dry and crisp to the touch. Make sure that the stems are completely dry, particularly at the top, otherwise the heads will soon droop. The drying time varies according to the conditions and type of plant, but it usually takes from one to four weeks.

Some plants, such as sea lavender and pampas grass, dry best standing upright in a jam jar or vase. Sand can be used to weight the jar and support the stems. Other plants should be placed in shallow water — about 5cm (2in) deep — to dry. Hydrangeas and gypsophilia dry best this way. Most grasses, fungi and twigs should be dried flat on an absorbent surface such as cardboard or newspaper. Leaves dried this way tend to shrivel but do not retain their natural colour. To prevent the seeds falling off grasses and cereals, and to give added strength to their stems, spray the plants with hair lacquer before, or even after, drying.

Flowers such as statice, larkspur and pearl achillea can be air dried. Hang them in small bunches, binding the stems first with rubber (elastic) bands.

Silica gel is used to preserve the shape and colour of roses. Carefully cover the flower with finely-ground crystals, being sure not to crush the petals.

DESICCANTS

Desiccants — or drying agents — draw moisture from the plants and help to preserve the natural colours and form of flowers. One of the simplest to use — though not the cheapest — is silica gel, which can be bought from most hardware stores or chemists. It usually comes in the form of white crystals which should be ground down to a finer grade before using. (Blue indicator crystals are also available — these turn pink when they have absorbed water.) Put a layer of crystals into the base of an air-tight container and place several wired flowerheads on top. Using a spoon, carefully cover the flowers with more of the desiccant, making sure that the crystals fall between the petals but do not misshape them. When the flowers are fully covered close the container and leave for a couple of days.

Borax is cheaper than silica gel, though it takes longer to work — at least ten days. Ideally it should be mixed with dry silver sand: three parts borax to two parts sand. Cover the flowers as with the silica gel.

GLYCERINE

A mixture of one part glycerine to two parts warm water is ideal for preserving the shape and suppleness of foliage. Either fully submerge the leaves in the solution (singly or in small sprays) or stand the stems of larger sprays in about 8-10cm (3-4in) of mixture. Cut the stems at a sharp angle and hammer the ends of woody stems to aid absorption. Gradually the glycerine will replace the water in the leaves. Submerged leaves take about two days, whereas plants left standing in the mixture take up to four weeks to dry; start checking after the first week.

Foliage, such as copper beech, can be preserved in a mixture of glycerine and water. This method stops the leaves from becoming brittle and misshapen.

Spray hair lacquer on to cereals and grasses to stop the stems wilting and the seeds falling off. You can do this either before or after drying.

EQUIPMENT

The picture opposite shows a range of equipment used in dried flower arranging. Certain items may only be required occasionally, as the need arises — wreath wrap for example is only used when making moss wreaths and garlands — whereas other items are considered essential; no flower arranger could cope for long without a strong pair of florists' scissors, a sharp knife, some wire and a block or two of florists' foam.

THE MECHANICS

The various items used to support the flowers in an arrangement are known as the mechanics. Florists' foam is the most popular mechanic. It comes in two forms: one for fresh flower arrangements (designed to absorb and hold water), the other for dried arrangements. The latter, often referred to as dry foam, comes in several shapes and sizes — spheres, blocks and cones — and can easily be cut down to any size or shape to fit a container.

Another much-used mechanic is wire mesh which is particularly good for larger, heavier arrangements. It can either be crumpled into a ball or other shape to fit inside the container or it can be packed with moss to form a more solid base. This latter method is sometimes used for making garlands and wreaths.

SECURING THE MECHANICS

It is sometimes possible to wedge the foam or wire mesh into a container so that it is held firm. But usually you will need to secure it in position. Florists' tape is very useful for attaching foam to the base of a container or, where necessary, for holding two or more pieces of foam together. Small plastic pinholders are also available for securing foam; they can be stuck down on to the container using fixative and the foam can then be pushed firmly on to the pins. Wire is used for attaching both foam and wire mesh to containers — particularly baskets where the wire can be threaded through the wicker work and the ends twisted together to secure.

Plaster of Paris is sometimes used in dried flower arranging to weight top heavy displays or support the mechanics — for example, when making a floral tree (see page 34).

Glue is sometimes used for sticking dry foam on to a container. It is also very useful for sticking plant materials together or gluing individual flowerheads or small posies on to a base, such as a box or a picture frame.

The equipment used in dried flower arranging includes: 1) Plaster of Paris; 2) dry foam; 3) a sharp knife; 4) strong florists' scissors; 5) wreath wrap; 6) string; 7) florists' tape; 8) fixative; 9) glue; 10) plastic pinholders; 11) reel rose wire; 12) black reel wire; 13) 15cm (6in) rose wire; 14, 15, and 16) stub wires; 17) wire mesh.

WIRE AND STRING

A variety of wire is used in dried flower arranging. Stub wires are straight lengths of wire that are generally used for supporting single flowerheads or binding together small groups of flowers (see page 14 for details). They are also used for supporting more unusual objects in an arrangement such as nuts, cones and so forth. The wires come in a range of different thicknesses, or gauges. Black reel wire is used for making moss wreaths and garlands, as these require a continuous length of wire (see pages 16-17). You can also buy reels of fine silver rose wire which is used for more delicate work, for example, for binding together posies (see page 49) or, in conjunction with string, for making small garlands (see page 105). Rose wire also comes in short lengths, about 15cm (6in) long. This can be used for binding miniature posies or wiring ribbon bows (see page 15).

CUTTING IMPLEMENTS

A strong pair of florists' scissors is essential for cutting plants down to size. Some scissors have a special wire-cutting edge; if yours do not, you will also require wire-cutters. Secateurs are useful for woody stems. A sharp knife is needed for stripping off unwanted leaves and branches from stems, and a second, longer knife is useful for slicing up large blocks of florists' foam.

BASIC TECHNIQUES

Some dried flowers — yarrow and larkspur for example — have strong, firm stems that need no support. Others, such as helichrysums, have weak stems that cannot withstand the weight of the flowerheads. In the latter case, wire can be used to support the flower. Cut a stem down to about 4cm (1½in) and place it against the end of a stub wire. Then bind the length of the stem to the wire using silver reel wire. (If you like, you can then cover and join the new 'stem' by binding gutta-percha tape around them.) This method can also be used for lengthening stems that are too short. For hollow-stemmed plants, such as safflowers and amaranthus, simply push a length of stub wire into the hollow end of the stem.

To increase the impact of colours in a display, flowers are frequently tied into small bunches before they are arranged. To do this, cut down the stems of two or three flowers — weak stems should be cut down to about 4cm (1½in); strong ones can be left longer. Take a length of stub wire and bend back the top 3-4cm (1-1½in) to form a hair-pin shape. Place the pin against the end of the stems, bent end towards the flowerheads. Then, starting about half way down the pin, begin to wind the long end of the wire around both the stems and the short end of the wire. Bind it about three times as shown below, then straighten it so that it forms a 'stem'. Trim the wire to the required length and insert it into the display.

Bows are frequently used to decorate dried flower arrangements. The easiest way to make a perfect bow is to wire it as described opposite. Other techniques used in dried flower arranging, such as making a garland or wreath, are described overleaf on pages 16-17.

To give flowers more impact in a display, wire them into small bunches before arranging them. First bend the end of a stub wire to form a hair-pin shape.

Cut the flower stems short and place them against the pin. Wind the long end of wire round about three times then straighten it to make a 'stem'.

Bows are often used to put the finishing touches to an arrangement. To make this double bow, take a length of satin ribbon about 60cm (2ft) long and make a loop at one end. Form a second loop as shown to make a bow shape. Ensure each time you loop the ribbon that you keep it right side out.

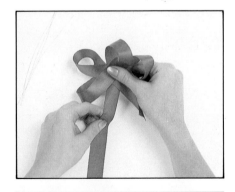

Loop the long tail over the front of the bow to form a third loop, and then to the back to make a fourth loop as shown.

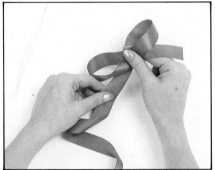

Wrap a length of rose wire round the centre of the bow and secure it by twisting the ends together. Use the ends of the wire to attach the bow to the arrangement. Now simply trim the tails to the required length, cutting them in a V-shape to finish off. This technique can easily be adapted to make a single bow or even a triple or quadruple one.

There are several ways of making a garland; this is but one of them. Another method is shown on page 63. Begin by taking some fresh, damp moss. Knead it to get rid of any large lumps, then roll it into a long cylindrical shape. Don't make the roll too thick as the flowers will eventually fatten it up.

Starting at one end, bind black reel wire tightly round the moss roll, keeping the turns quite close together. Trim off any straggly pieces of moss as you go.

Allow the garland to dry before inserting the flowers. These should be wired in small bunches and inserted at an acute angle into the moss rather than at right angles. A variation on this method, often used for larger garlands, is to roll the moss out on top of a length of wire mesh. You then roll the moss up in the mesh and turn the raw edges of wire under to secure it.

To make a wreath such as this you need a wire wreath frame and some dry moss. Knead the moss to get rid of any lumps then pack a handful into the frame.

Attach some black reel wire to the frame and, working in an anti-clockwise direction, begin to bind the moss-filled frame, pulling tightly with each turn. Continue to pack and bind the moss into the frame until the whole wreath is complete.

If you like, you can cover the ring with plastic wreath wrap. Attach one end of the wrap to the ring using a wire pin then wind the wrap around the wreath as shown. Wire the flowers into small bunches and insert them into the wreath. Another way to make a wreath is to create a garland as described opposite: then bend it into a ring and secure the ends with wire.

Helichrysum
(Strawflower or everlasting)

Acroclinium
(also Helipterum — sunray)

Rosa
(Rose)

Helichrysum
(South African daisy)

Achillea
(Lonas — a type of yarrow)

Xeranthemum

Limonium sinuatum
(Statice)

Delphinium
(Larkspur)

Limonium tataricum
(Sea lavender)

Lavandula
(Lavender)

Hydrangea

Solidago
(Golden rod)

Physalis
(Chinese lantern)

Papaver
(Poppy seedheads)

Amaranthus
(Love-lies-bleeding)

Lagarus
(Rabbit's or hare's tail grass)

Lunaria
(Honesty)

Phalaris
(Reed grass)

Hordeum
(Black-eared barley)

Avena fatua
(Wild oats)

LAVENDER FAIR

A combination of lavender and red
helichrysum form a delightful
surround for this small basket of pot-
pourri. Begin by wiring small
bunches of lavender — about three
to four stems each. Attach a bunch
to the rim of the basket by wrapping
the wire through the wicker work.
Position the next bunch over the
stems of the first to cover the wires.
Continue round the rim.

When the rim is fully covered, cover
the handle in the same way. Add a
splash of colour to the display with
wired bunches of small red
helichrysum (everlasting or
strawflower). Attach them at
intervals to the rim of the basket,
using the same method as before. Put
two more bunches on the handle.

Make a single bow out of deep red
ribbon, wiring it together as
described on page 15. Attach the
bow to the middle of the handle and
cover the wire with a strand of
lavender; fix this in place using fine
silver rose wire. To finish, fill the
basket with pot-pourri, choosing a
type that complements the colours of
the arrangement.

The same basket as the one used opposite but a completely different design — here, netting has been used to create a soft billowing effect. Wire together clumps of red amaranthus (love-lies-bleeding) and insert them at intervals around the rim of the basket. Keep the angles irregular so that some stems are standing up, others hanging down.

Fill in with clumps of blue larkspur and soft pink *Helichrysum casianum*, forming a dense ring of flowers around the basket.

Take three strips of lilac netting and form single bows, wiring them as described on page 15. Attach bows to the base of the handle on either side and put the third one in the middle as shown. Finally, fill the basket with sweet-smelling pot-pourri.

To create this vibrant design, first make a moss base for the basket. Roll some wire mesh into a tube, pack it with dry moss and close the ends. Squash the base into the basket and wire it in place as shown. Begin to form the outline of the arrangement with bleached white helichrysum (strawflower or everlasting), creating a dome shape.

Continue to build up the shape with white proteus. Add some clubrush next, followed by a number of cones, such as these meridianum. The colour of these two plants cleverly picks up the brown in the basket.

Complete the display with bright yellow clumps of cressia and cluster-flowered helichrysum. Place them low down in the arrangement, filling in the gaps between the other plants.

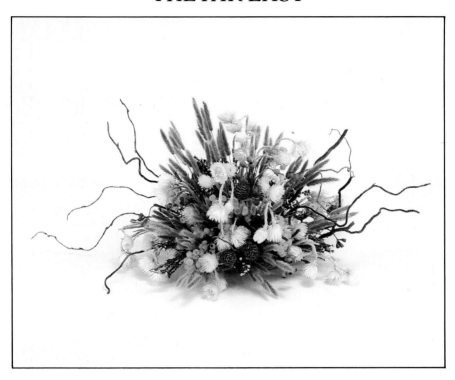

A few gnarled twigs give this attractive arrangement an oriental quality. Begin by making a moss base. Mould some wire mesh into a tube, fill it with dry moss and close the ends. Pack this into a small wicker basket, securing it with wire. Now insert a few twisted willow twigs, mainly at the sides, to form an unusual shape. Add some white proteus next, and a few grasses.

Use the grass to form the main outline, keeping the stems quite tall at the back. Put some shorter stems in the foreground, so that they hang over the edge of the basket. Now begin to fill in with small yellow helichrysum (strawflower or everlasting). Arrange the flowers low down, deep in amongst the other plants.

Add highlights to the display with a few wired clumps of bleached white helichrysum. The bleaching tends to make the heads drop which adds to the charm of the arrangement. For contrasting textures, add a few cones and finish off with stems of bobbly canella.

Bring a touch of the country into your living room with this beautiful array of garden flowers. Take a wicker shopping basket and fill the top with wire mesh, attaching the mesh to the sides of the basket with wire. Form a base for the arrangement by packing the mesh with wired bunches of sea lavender.

Wire clumps of love-in-a-mist and insert them into the arrangement so that they stand out above the sea lavender. Then start to fill in with bunches of soft pink larkspur. Try to keep the arrangement slightly parted around the handle so that the latter is not totally obscured.

Finish filling in with bunches of lady's mantle. This, along with the larkspur, gives the arrangement a soft and gentle quality. Add several garden roses to complete the picture.

A small wicker basket holds a cheerful display of tiny flowers. Begin by packing the base of the basket with wire mesh, wiring it to the rim to hold it in position. Fix the lid open using a piece of thick wire as a prop. Now form a base for the display using sea lavender, arranging it loosely throughout the mesh.

Fill in the display with wired clumps of yellow silver-leaved helichrysum, keeping it tight and slightly lower than the sea lavender. Add a splash of colour with small clumps of red helichrysum, breaking out of the shape a little with some taller pieces at the back.

Add groups of small red roses, concentrating them in groups, some bursting out of the sides of the arrangement, others spilling over the front. A few poppy heads add contrast of texture — insert about three bunches, keeping them tall so that they stand out above the other flowers. Finish off with stems of brown 'blue leaf', fanning them out on one side as shown above.

A collection of brilliantly coloured flowers makes a striking display for the sideboard. Begin by moulding some wire mesh into a three-dimensional shape, keeping the base flat and the top end open. Pack the mesh with dry moss, then close up the open end. Now insert wired bunches of stirlingia — tall, upright stems at the top, shorter, horizontal ones lower down.

Next, arrange a few stems of blue larkspur around the top, and shorter bunches of blue statice lower down, following the general pattern set by the stirlingia. Follow with wired bunches of pink-dyed quaking grass, breaking out of the outline, and a few clumps of blue-dyed *Leucodendron brunia.*

Once you are happy with the general shape of the arrangement, start to fill in with bunches of large pink helichrysum (strawflower or everlasting). Pack them deep into the display. Add bright yellow highlights next with bunches of cluster-flowered helichrysum.

Finally, wire together a few bunches of rich red roses and scatter them throughout the display. It is important to position the roses last, because this ensures that the heads remain well exposed.

In this attractive design, contrasting colours and textures combine to create a delightful picture. Take a small wicker basket and fill it with wire mesh, attaching the mesh at intervals to the side of the basket with wire. Start to build up the outline of the display using single lengths of blue larkspur.

Complete the outline with wired bunches of sea holly, keeping the shape full and wide. Next, fill in with bunches of large pink helichrysum (strawflower or everlasting). Keep them shorter than the other plants so that they lie lower down in the arrangement.

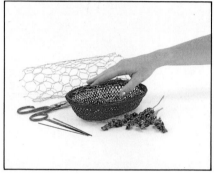

Finally, pick out the colour of the basket with bunches of bright pink rabbit's or hare's tail grass, scattering them throughout the arrangement and bringing it to life.

A dark, rustic basket cradles a wild and colourful display of plants. Begin by placing a large block of florists' foam inside the basket. Run a couple of wires across the top to hold the foam in place, securing the ends of the wires to the rim of the basket.

Build up the outline of the display with wired clumps of love-in-a-mist, allowing some of the flowerheads to droop over the sides of the basket. Next, slot in single stems of bottlebrush at varying heights to give rich red tones to the display.

Add bright yellow highlights by inserting wired clumps of yarrow throughout. Finally, arrange some long stems of blue larkspur, keeping them slightly taller than the other plants.

Co-ordinate a floral display with your curtains or soft furnishings by covering the base in some matching fabric. Take a piece of left-over material and wrap it round a suitable basket. Pack the inside of the basket with wire mesh and hold it in place using strips of wire pushed through both the fabric and the wicker work.

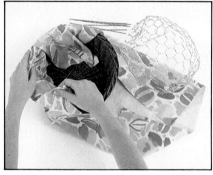

Wire bunches of beige cluster-flowered sunray and bright yellow yarrow and pack them tightly into the wire mesh, forming a dome-shaped outline. Now scatter several wired bunches of reed grass throughout the arrangement.

Add large wired bunches of lavender next, keeping the stems long so that the flowers stand out above the other plants. Finish off with groups of South African daisies (a type of helichrysum). These plants have been chosen to match the colours in the fabric so, when you follow this design, alter the range of flowers according to your colour scheme.

An old bicycle basket makes the perfect container for this delightfully random display of flowers. First, fill the top of the basket with wire mesh, attaching it to the sides with reel wire threaded through the wicker. Now begin to build up the outline using tall stems of blue larkspur.

Fill in the shape using fluffy white gypsophilia (baby's breath) and clumps of flowering love-in-a-mist, positioning the plants lower down in the arrangement and keeping them well scattered.

The focal flowers in the display are pretty pink and yellow acroclinium (sunray). Arrange large clumps of them throughout, keeping the heads well exposed. Finish off with a ring of hydrangea around the rim of the basket. This helps to lift the other flowers and forms an effective link between the basket and the display.

This wild arrangement is designed to look like a freshly-gathered basket of flowers and grasses. Use a basket with a low 'lip' at one end and put a ball of wire mesh at the taller end; secure it with wire. Now arrange several large clumps of oats, keeping those at the front long so that they overhang the lip, those further back becoming shorter and more upright.

Now intersperse the oats with wired bunches of love-in-a-mist, maintaining the general shape, with long low-lying stems at the front, shorter upright ones at the back. Follow these with bunches of small poppy seedheads, arranged mainly towards the front of the display so that they appear to be spilling out over the lip. Add a few larger poppy seedheads as well for contrast.

Arrange clumps of sea holly next, sprinkling them throughout. They add an interesting hint of blue to the neutral tones of the arrangement. Now add a dramatic contrast in shape and texture with some large globe thistle heads. Concentrate these around the handle, pushing some deep into the arrangement, and then place a few long stems in the foreground.

Soften the whole arrangement by adding a few grasses and then finish off by placing several lotus seedheads at the back, using them to cover any exposed wire mesh.

This ever-popular form of floral arrangement is not as difficult to achieve as you might think. Begin by selecting a suitable container for the base. Mix up some plaster of Paris with water and fill the container. Quickly insert an interestingly-shaped branch for the stem, holding it in position for a couple of minutes until the plaster begins to set.

Next, make a ring of wire mesh, slightly deeper than the container and wide enough to fit snuggly round it. The ring must be double thickness so you can pack it with dry moss. When it is fully packed, neatly bend the raw edges of wire over to close the ring. Now cut several equal lengths of birch twigs and attach them to the moss ring using wire pins — two per twig.

Cover the wire pins by tying long strands of raffia around the ring. Once the plaster has set, place the container inside the wire surround. Take a large sphere of florists' foam and scrape out the centre using a knife. Press the ball on to the wooden 'stem' of the tree, making sure it is held firm. Now wire some small bunches of flowers, leaving at least 3cm (1in) of wire 'tail'.

The flowers used here are orange and yellow helichrysum (strawflower or everlasting), blue larkspur and green amaranthus (love-lies-bleeding). Use the helichrysum first to form the shape, keeping the arrangement spherical. Next add the larkspur and amaranthus, making sure they do not protrude too far out of the arrangement and break up the shape.

Finish off by putting pieces of moss around the base of the tree to hide the plaster of Paris and the wire mesh.

A jet black wooden box provides a frame for this pretty arrangement, and helps to bring out the subtle warmth of the roses. Cut a block of florists' foam to fit the box and wedge it tightly in place. If the fit is good there should be no need to tape it.

Build up the outline using wired bunches of white bupleurum. Keep the shape well within that of the box. Start to fill in the outline with South African daisies (a type of helichrysum), using them to cover the foam. Make the flowers shorter at the front of the display, slightly overhanging the edge of the box.

Complete the picture with several rust-coloured roses, recessing some deep into the arrangement. Gently pull back the outer petals if necessary to open out the flowers before you position them.

This dark and moody arrangement makes an interesting change from the more usual brightly coloured displays. It is set within a shiny black plastic box designed for office use. Begin by packing two circular pieces of florists' foam into the box — this will give height to the centre of the arrangement. Next build up the shape with reed.

Add a hint of red with long stems of rat's tail statice scattered in amongst the reed. Try to keep the height of the two plants about the same.

Wire together clumps of South African daisies (a type of helichrysum) and insert them deep into the arrangement. These add welcome highlights to the display and bring it to life.

A host of tiny flowers and grasses cluster round an old but gleaming brass bell, creating a very pretty effect. Cut a slice from a cylinder of florists' foam then cut the slice in half. Gouge out the centre of the two halves and affix the pieces to the handle as shown, using tape.

Build up the shape of the arrangement using single stems of mauve xeranthemum. Position those at the top of the display upright, and those lower down dangling over the bell. Now intersperse with wired clumps of quaking grass, following the same outline. Finish off with bunches of lady's mantle, pushed well into the arrangement.

Brass cow bells have been used to create this unusual display. Bind together several small bunches of flowers with silver wire. The pink bunch consists of gypsophilia (baby's breath) and acroclinium (sunray); the yellow of oats, love-in-a-mist, and cluster-flowered helichrysum. Glue the bunches on to the bells, covering up the wires with short lengths of coloured cord.

Alternatively, you can glue the flowerheads directly on to the bell in a ring as shown here. These flowers are yellow helichrysum filled in with golden rod. Finally, tie a length of cord to one or more bells for hanging. Tie an extra little bunch of gypsophilia half way up the cord for an added touch.

A wooden biscuit barrel sets off an unusually dark arrangement of plants to perfection. First pack the barrel with a length of wire mesh.

Build up a fan-shaped outline using stems of *Leucodendron,* then fill in the remaining gaps with clumps of red berzilia. The stems of both plants are fairly strong so there should be no need to wire them.

Finally, add some stems of apricot glabrum cones, positioning them mainly in the centre of the arrangement to act as the focal point. Keep the stems short so that they sit deep in amongst the other plants, giving substance to the display.

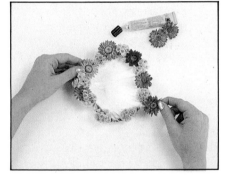

Brighten up dishes of nuts and candies at party-time with a few dried flowers. For the candy dish, take a clam shell and dab glue on to the rim. Then take a number of heads of yellow anaphalis (pearl everlasting) and stick them in groups at regular intervals around the rim.

Fill in the gaps between the yellow anaphalis with bright pink heads of acroclinium (sunray). The flowers used here have been chosen to match the colour of the candies — in this case sugared almonds. For different coloured candies, chose your own selection of flowers. The wooden bowl containing the nuts has been decorated in exactly the same way. This time, the flowers chosen are South African daisies (a type of helichrysum), beige cluster-flowered sunray and clubrush. As before, the choice of plant reflects the colours of the contents of the dish.

A giant brandy glass spills over with a lovely display of flowers. First, fill the glass with pot-pourri. Next make a moss-filled mushroom shape out of wire mesh, ensuring that the cap is large enough to sit on the rim of the glass. Make the 'mushroom' by moulding wire mesh into a bowl shape and half filling it with moss. Then gather the spare wire together at the top to form a 'stalk'.

Sit the 'mushroom' on top of the brandy glass. Insert wired bunches of grey stirlingia into the moss, building up an even, rounded shape. Now wire together clumps of blue larkspur and dot these in amongst the stirlingia, keeping the shape consistent.

Add highlights to the arrangement with cream anaphalis (pearl everlasting), putting it deep down in amongst the other flowers and covering up any part of the glass rim still showing. Finally, add about 20 small red roses, dotting them singly throughout, and bringing the display to life.

GINGERBREAD MEN

Put a small biscuit tin to use as a flower container and make a cheerful display for the kitchen. Begin by cutting a block of florists' foam small enough to fit inside the tin, leaving a space free at one end for the gingerbread men. Half fill the empty end with tissue paper — this will help prevent the biscuits becoming damaged.

Wire small clumps of South African daisy (a form of helichrysum) and arrange them in the foam, keeping them to one side of the tin.

Now add several clumps of red berzilia, filling in any gaps. Place the five gingerbread men at varying heights and angles into the free end of the tin. Finish off by popping a few last stems of flowers in amongst the biscuits so that the gingerbread men are just peeping out.

In this striking arrangement, a selection of natural coloured flowers and grasses has been chosen to complement the copper colours of the kettle. To begin, crush some wire mesh into a ball and place it inside the receptacle. Then build up the outline using plenty of black-eared barley.

Intersperse the arrangement with bleached white helichrysum (strawflower or everlasting) — these will add a welcome contrast to the browns and help to bring the display alive. Then add a few stems of moon grass.

To finish, add stems of clubrush throughout, recessing them deep into the arrangement to create depth. Try to keep the whole display light and airy with a slightly spiky effect.

Transform your fruit bowl with an unusual floral display. In this arrangement, gold and russets have been chosen to reflect the colour of both bowl and fruit. Begin by rolling a length of wire mesh into a tube about 3cm (1in) in diameter and fixing it into one half of the bowl. Now place wired bunches of dudinea into the mesh to build up the shape.

Wire together a few groups of Chinese lantern — about four to five heads per group — and place these in amongst the dudinea.

Add about two to three wired bunches of millet, allowing them to droop across the arrangement and over the sides of the bowl. You don't need to use many stems to get the desired effect. Finally, put the fruit into the bowl, adding a last piece of dudinea at the front to complete the picture.

A n old iron that hasn't seen a board for many a day is given a second lease of life as part of an imaginative floral arrangement. Cut a slice off a cylinder of florists' foam and attach it to the iron with a narrow strip of florists' tape. Begin to build up the shape of the display using wired clumps of lady's mantle.

Next, add small bunches of blue larkspur, evenly dotted throughout the arrangement. Follow with clumps of pink miniature sunray, pushing some of them deep into the display.

To finish, add clumps of bold yellow button chrysanthemums, putting them mainly around the edges of the arrangement, and using them to fill in any gaps, and cover any tape still exposed.

A battered old shovel that has seen better days makes a novel setting for this brightly coloured display. Begin by cutting a section from a cylinder of florists' foam and taping it on to the base of the shovel. Form an outline using stems of golden rod then fill in with yarrow, positioning the latter deeper down in the arrangement to cover the foam.

To contrast the bright yellow of the yarrow, dot some dark oak leaves throughout the display. Then form a ring of leaves around the base. Add highlights with a few clumps of creamy helichrysum (strawflower or everlasting).

Finally, bring the arrangement fully alive with several groups of Chinese lantern. Push them deep down so that they peep out from amongst the other plants.

FLOWER SIEVE

An old flour sieve provides a frame for this pretty front-facing design. Cut a sphere of florists' foam in two and tape one half on to the side of the sieve. Build up a spiky outline using ears of wheat, pushing them singly into the foam. Keep the arrangement asymmetrical by making the stems longer on one side so that they spill out of the bottom of the 'frame'.

Follow the general outline already created using pink larkspur, keeping it as tall as the wheat. Intersperse the arrangement with South African daisies (a type of helichrysum). Place them at varying heights, then add depth with several bunches of moon grass, pushing them well into the display.

Complete the picture with a small posy on top of the sieve; wire together a small group of plants, then cover the wire with raffia. Finish off with a bow and glue the posy on to the sieve.

A n old wooden bread board, some bread sticks and an array of flowers and grasses makes an original decoration for the kitchen. First drill a hole in the board about 3cm (1in) away from the edge. Thread a length of raffia through the hole and tie three bread sticks on to the board.

Next, make a posy out of small pink helichrysum (strawflower or everlasting), red berzilia and beard grass as follows. Wire together a tall group of plants using a long piece of silver wire. Add a second, slightly shorter, group to the bunch and bind it as before. Continue to add progressively shorter groups to the posy, binding at each stage with the same length of wire.

With the raffia, tie a second bundle of bread sticks to the board, at right angles to the first. Then tie the posy in position, finishing off with a raffia bow.

This battered old watering can has been given a new lease of life as part of an imaginative arrangement of flowers, cereals and grasses. Begin by packing wire mesh into the neck of the can.

Start to build up the shape of the display with tall bundles of black-earled barley, putting them both sides of the handle. It is not necessary to wire the barley. Next scatter purple xeranthemums throughout, keeping some stems quite short, others as tall as the barley.

Continue to fill out the display using plenty of yellow-dyed rabbit's or hare's tail grass. Add the grass singly and concentrate it around the base of the arrangement so that it helps to cover the top of the watering can. Add depth to the display with long stems of brown 'blue leaf', following the general outline.

When you are happy with the shape of the arrangement, put a few xeranthemums and ears of barley into the spout so that they look as if they are spilling out. To finish, plait three lengths of raffia. Using an extra strand of raffia, fix the plait into a bow shape and tie it on to the handle of the watering can.

A stoneware hot water bottle holds a pretty display of flowers. Begin by slicing a sphere of florists' foam in half and gouging out the centre of one piece with a knife. Push this foam over the opening of the bottle so that it fits snugly and is held firmly in place. Now wire several bunches of daisy-like rhodanthe (sunray) and insert them into the foam.

Once you have formed the outline, fill the centre of the display with three dryandra; push them deep down in amongst the rhodanthe. Finish off with a few wired groups of bright yellow yarrow to add a splash of colour.

The flowers in this quaint design have been specially chosen to blend with the rusty tones of the terracotta pot. Start by packing wire mesh into the base of the pot, leaving about 1cm (½in) protruding from the top. Put the lid at a rakish angle over two-thirds of the pot, making sure it is well balanced.

Wire small bunches of South African daisy (a form of helichrysum) and push them into the mesh. Next add wired bunches of peachy cluster-flowered sunray, filling in the arrangement.

Finally, add stems of pink-dyed *Leucodendron brunia* throughout, pushing some deep into the arrangement, keeping others long so that the bobbly heads break through the outline and hang over the sides of the pot.

Acouple of old wooden spoons
form the basis of a pretty
arrangement that would brighten up
any kitchen. First, wire the spoons
together at an angle as shown,
winding the wire round the handles
several times to secure firmly.

Wire together several small groups
of plants, choosing an attractive
range of colours. Shown here is
yellow quaking grass, white
helichrysum (strawflower or
everlasting) and dudinea seedheads.
Wire the small groups together to
form one large bunch and attach this
to the spoons so that the blooms sit
prettily over the bowls.

Make a large bright double bow out
of satin ribbon, following the
instructions on page 15, and tie it
with a second length of ribbon
around the spoons and the posy.

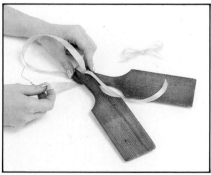

A pair of butter pats makes an unusual setting for this kitchen design. Take a length of ribbon and wire up one end. Thread the ribbon through both holes from the front, leaving a long tail between the pats. Loop the ribbon over the top and thread through from the front again, pulling it tight. Make a second loop in the same way, leaving it long for hanging the display.

Secure the wired end of ribbon at the back with a knot; cut off any excess. Wire a small bow on to the front of the pats. Then attach half a sphere of florists' foam to the ribbon 'tail' using tape. Wire small bunches of blue jasilda and tiny red helichrysum and push them into the ball, packing them tightly together.

Add longer stems of blue larkspur, leaving some pieces trailing down the pats to break up the outline of the ball. Finally, wire up short double loops of ribbon and intersperse them among the flowers, finishing off with a couple of longer strands at the bottom.

The framework of this seasonal garland is made of cones and walnuts. Wire the cones by wrapping stub wire around the base. For the walnuts, push stub wire through one end as far as it will go. Take a group of cones and nuts and twist the wires together. Add to the base of the group and twist the wires again to secure. Continue in this way until the garland is long enough.

Make a double bow out of gold gift wrap ribbon (following the instructions on page 15) and wire two extra tails on to it. (Just fold a length of ribbon in half for the tails and wire in the middle.) Attach the bow to one end of the garland, then wire a long length of ribbon to the same end. Wrap this through the garland, twisting it round the cones. Leave a long tail at the far end.

To finish, wire together small groups of bright Chinese lanterns and bunches of quaking grass. Intersperse them amongst the cones, entangling the wires to secure them.

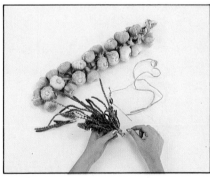

Not as sweet smelling perhaps as some of the other arrangements, but certainly very useful. First make a tied bunch of flowers as follows. Bind a small group of flowers with a length of reel wire. Gradually add more flowers to the bunch, binding them with the same length of wire, until the posy is the desired size.

The flowers used here are rat's tail statice and dryandra. Tie a length of raffia round the end of the posy and finish off with a bow. Wire the posy on to the end of a purchased garland of garlic bulbs. Complete the picture by wiring about five large protea heads and binding them on to the garland in amongst the garlic.

This aromatic pomander contains a range of interesting spices and makes an unusual kitchen decoration. Begin by plaiting three strands of raffia. Join the ends with a long piece of wire, then push the wire through a sphere of florists' foam, doubling it back on itself to secure. Wire bunches of cinnamon and Spanish root (liquorice stick) and conceal the wires with thin strands of raffia.

The other two spices used are star-shaped aniseed and white lomius. Wire these also and cover the foam with the spices, trying to keep the shape roughly spherical. Now insert clumps of small poppy heads, filling in the gaps between the spices.

Add some large poppy heads for contrast. Insert them singly but arrange them in groups of two or three, standing out from the other plants. Finally, add a few dark cones to add depth to the arrangement — those used here are platyspernum cones.

A small block of cork bark forms the base for an attractive display of neutral-coloured plants. Begin by cutting a piece of florists' foam down to a size that will sit comfortably on the middle of the bark. Tape the foam in place.

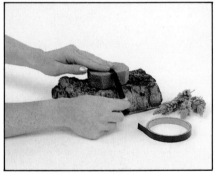

Build up the outline of the display with single stems of green amaranthus (love-lies-bleeding). Create a spiky effect, with some of the plants trailing over the edges of the bark. Fill in with *Leucodendron,* keeping the stems shorter than those of the amaranthus so that the plants lie lower down in the arrangement.

To finish, add a few highlights with several small wire bunches of ammobium (sandflower), concentrating them in the centre of the display.

Alarge piece of bark forms part of a colourful display of oranges, creams and browns. Choose a piece of bark with a good shape and interesting, gnarled features. Start by moulding some wire mesh into a tube and filling it with moss. Attach this to the bark using lengths of wire. Bore small holes in the sides of the bark to secure the wire if necessary.

Begin to build up the shape of the arrangement using wired clumps of dudinea. Scatter them throughout the moss base, keeping the shape low and well within the outline of the bark. Next add clumps of bright yellow cluster-flowered helichrysum (strawflower or everlasting), followed by groups of bobbly *Leucodendron brunia*.

Wire together bunches of large helichrysum, choosing a range of colours, and use these to fill in the arrangement, still keeping the shape low and compact. For contrast, add stems of brown 'blue leaf', allowing some to break out of the outline.

To soften the effect, arrange clumps of golden rod throughout. Then finish off with a few wired stems of oats.

W ood always provides a perfect setting for dried flowers, and an old wooden plane makes a particularly attractive display. Cut a block of florists' foam and wedge it tightly into the hole. Arrange wired clumps of cluster-flowered sunray first, keeping the outline low. Follow with pink *Leucodendron brunia,* allowing it to break out of the shape and dangle low over the sides.

Now add interest and a dash of colour with a few stems of bottlebrush. Put them in singly and keep them short so that their rich colour lies deep within the arrangement.

Soften the effect with a few clumps of grass interspersed throughout. To finish, add contrasting texture with three or four heads of *Leucodendron plumosum* set deep into the display.

An old cotton spool is transformed by a lively display of bright yellow flowers. Make a garland of flowers as follows. Attach some reel wire to a length of string, about 20cm (8in) from one end. Position a small group of flowers against the join and wrap the wire round the stems to secure. Put another group of flowers over the stems of the first and secure as before.

Continue in this way until the garland is long enough to go round the spool. The flowers used here are brilliant yellow helichrysum (strawflower or everlasting), white larkspur and fluffy golden morrison. Attach the garland to the base of the spool by tying the string round it. Wrap the garland round the spool and secure at the top with the other end of the string.

A miniature chest of drawers makes a lovely setting for a display of dried flowers. Begin by packing the drawers with florists' foam, putting larger pieces in the bottom drawer and smaller pieces higher up.

Start to fill the drawers with flowers, keeping the fullest arrangement in the bottom drawer to balance the design. First pack a few wired bunches of miniature sunray into the drawers. Then add bunches of South African daisies (a type of helichrysum); two different colours have been used here — white and golden.

Fill in with wired bunches of yarrow and finally, fluffy clumps of small yellow helichrysum (strawflower or everlasting).

FLORAL BOOK ENDS

B righten up a pair of dull book ends with a cheerful floral display. Begin by fixing some florists' foam to the base of the book end using florists' tape.

Form the basic outline of the display using brown clubrush, following the shape of the book end. Then begin to fill in with yellow silver-leaved helichrysum (strawflower or everlasting), pushing it deep into the arrangement.

Complete the display by interspersing some red helichrysum and pink miniature sunray throughout. Repeat with the other book end, balancing this second arrangement with the first.

An old clock is given a new lease of life with a pretty garland of flowers. First, cover the top of the clock with strips of wreath wrap (alternatively, use cellophane, cling film or plastic wrap), attaching them to the clock with fine silver wire. This will protect the wood from becoming damaged.

Cut two long strips of wire mesh and roll them into tubes about 3cm (1in) in diameter. Attach the tubes to the clock over the protective cover, using reel wire to secure them. Keep one wire tube forward, draping it round to the front of the clock at the base; the other tube positioned further back.

Now begin to cover the wire mesh by inserting small clumps of larkspur and moon grass. Intersperse these with wired bunches of yellow helichrysum (strawflower or everlasting) to add a splash of colour. Make sure that the flowers are tightly packed so that they hide the wrap and do not obscure the clock face.

Finally, pick up the rich tones of the wood with rust coloured nipplewort (or broom bloom), placing small clumps throughout the arrangement.

FLOWER POT GARLAND

To make this attractive design you must start by constructing a garland of flowers. Take a length of string and secure some black reel wire to it some distance from the end. Place a small bunch of flowers over the join and bind it in position with the wire. Keep adding plants in this way, each time covering the stems of the previous bunch.

The flowers used in this garland are miniature sunray and South African daisies (a type of helichrysum). Once the garland is long enough, attach it to the pot using an all-purpose adhesive. Tie the ends of the string together at the back and cut off any excess. Now put your favourite plant inside. (Be careful when watering it not to spill any on the flowers).

Don't throw away that old broken flower pot — transform it instead into a stunning autumnal arrangement using black-eared barley and bright yellow helichrysum (strawflower or everlasting). Wedge a piece of florists' foam into the broken pot and secure it with tape. Now build up the shape of the arrangement with the barley, putting the discarded stems to one side.

Place longer stems of barley into the base of the display and generally shorter ones at the top, around the rim. Intersperse the barley with cluster-flowered helichrysum, placing the heads deep in the arrangement. Concentrate the yellow around the rim of the pot to cover up any foam still visible.

Run a line of helichrysum around the broken edge of the pot, pushing the stems into the foam or gluing the heads on if necessary. Finally, take the discarded barley stems and cut off the ends at a sharp angle. Now position them at the back of the display, splaying them out so that they appear to be continuous with the stems at the front.

A beautiful old china jug, bursting with sheaves of oats, makes a striking arrangement for the hallway. Begin by making a garland of flowers to fit round the neck of the jug. Construct the frame of the garland using moss and reel wire, following the instructions given in detail on page 16. Leave long tails of wire at either end of the garland.

When the frame is completed, mould a piece of wire mesh into a ball and put it into the jug.

Wrap the moss frame round the neck of the jug and secure it in position by twisting the free ends of the wire together. Select some flowers that co-ordinate with the colours in the jug. Used here are pale blue helichrysum (strawflower or everlasting), blue-dyed achillea and pearl achillea (two types of yarrow).

Wire the flowers into small bunches and insert them into the garland, pushing the wires in at a slight angle rather than at right angles. Arrange the different types alternately, packing them close together to form a thick ring of flowers all the way round the jug.

To complete the display, cut a large amount of oats down to the same height and push them, a bundle at a time, into the wire mesh ball at the base of the jug. Make sure they are packed very tightly and stand straight.

A beautiful old tobacco pot makes a perfect setting for a striking display of brightly coloured flowers. Note how the blue and orange in the china have been picked up by the colours of the flowers. First, cut a block of florists' foam to fit snugly inside the pot.

Using wired bunches of helichrysum (strawflower or everlasting), build up a dome shape to reflect the shape of the pot. Then add clusters of blue-dyed *Leucodendron brunia.* The unusual bobbly shape of this plant will always add interest to any arrangement.

Finally, add clumps of bright yellow morrison to fill in any gaps and complete the display.

A giant Minton cup and saucer doubles up as a pot-pourri container. The same effect can easily be created with a normal-sized cup and saucer, using smaller-headed flowers. Make a cylinder out of wire mesh and bend it into a ring large enough to fit around the base of the cup. Knot the ends of the wire together.

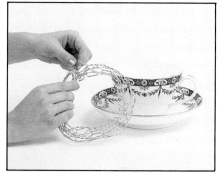

Wire several bunches of deep pink helichrysum (strawflower or everlasting), blue-dyed cluster-flowered sunray and creamy cauliflower. Slot them alternately into the mesh, packing them in tightly to cover the wire but being sure not to obscure the pattern on the side of the cup.

Once the 'garland' has been completed, you can fill the cup with pot-pourri, choosing a mixture that complements the colours of the arrangement.

A classic willow pattern vegetable dish serves up an exciting Oriental display of flowers and curling tallscreen. Begin by cutting a block of florists' foam to fit inside the dish. Secure the foam with florists' tape as shown. Prop the lid up against the dish, leaving three quarters of the foam exposed.

Start to build up the general shape of the arrangement using wired clumps of helichrysum (strawflower or everlasting). Then fill in with large bunches of yarrow, covering most of the foam. Keep the shape low and within the outline of the dish.

Add a complete contrast of colour and texture with several stems or tallscreen — their fascinating shape adds interest to any arrangement. Place them at various angles, keeping them taller than the other plants so that they are clearly visible.

Finish off with a few stems of flowering love-in-a-mist, arranging them so that they break out of the general, low-lying outline. The faint hint of blue in these flowers picks up the blue in the dish.

A ball of colourful flowers adds a welcome splash of colour to an old wooden lamp stand. Begin by slicing a sphere of florists' foam in half and cutting away the centre of each half so that the pieces fit snugly around the stand. Tape the two halves in position as shown.

Wire the flowers into small bunches; used here are blue larkspur, small yellow helichrysum (strawflower or everlasting), green amaranthus (love-lies-bleeding) and dudinea. Insert the plants into the foam, keeping the shape spherical. Position the more spiky larkspur and amaranthus first, then fill in with the dudinea and helichrysum.

A striking and imaginative display transforms a plain lampshade. Begin by wiring together three bunches of flowers, carefully selecting plants that blend well with the colour of your shade. The plants shown here are helichrysum (strawflower or everlasting), cluster-flowered sunray and rat's tail statice.

Make three small holes at the base of the shade. Attach the bunches on to the shade by threading the wires through the holes and securing them at the back. Position the middle bunch upright and the ones on either side running parallel with the rim. Make sure the ends are packed closely together so that none of the stems or wires is showing.

This attractive design illustrates how much a floral arrangement can enhance a plain picture frame — it's easy to do but so very effective. Cut a slice of florists' foam to fit one corner of the frame and tape it in place. Begin to loosely build up the shape using single stems of clubrush.

Add a splash of colour throughout the display with bright yellow cressia, allowing some to trail across the frame and picture. Then insert a number of single stems of bottlebrush to add interest and colour.

Fill out the display with plenty of bottlebrush foliage. Then add highlights with a few white leaf skeletons such as these peepal leaves.

Finally, make a double bow out of tartan ribbon, following the instructions on page 15. Attach this to the lower portion of the arrangement so that the long tails of the bow trail across the frame. Repeat the whole procedure on the opposite corner, being sure to keep the design well balanced.

Bring an old frame to life with this attractive arrangement of oats and flowers. Cut four lengths of wire mesh, making them slightly longer than the sides of the frame. Roll them up into tubes about 3cm (1in) in diameter and fix them tightly round the frame, joining them at the corners with wire.

Wire large clumps of oats and pack them tightly into the wire mesh frame so that the strands become entangled and hold each other together. The oats provide a good base for the other plants and help to keep them in place. Now add wired bunches of yellow anaphalis (pearl everlasting), arranging them at intervals around the frame.

Position wired bunches of pink *Helichrysum casianum* in amongst the oats, keeping them close to the anaphalis. Finish off with several groups of blue *Leucodendron brunia*, their rich, dark colour adding contrast to the arrangement.

I n this attractive design, the dried flowers form the picture rather than the frame. Take a small oval frame and remove the glass, leaving only the backing board. Cut the heads off a colourful selection of plants and start to glue them on to the board. Begin with a red rose in the middle, surrounded by bright yellow yarrow. Add red celosia cockscomb next.

Continue to arrange the heads in small groups, covering the entire surface. The other plants used here are love-in-a-mist heads inside bells of Ireland, lotus seedheads and silver bobbles of *Leucodendron brunia*. The picture is completed with some pearl achillea (a type of yarrow) dotted in amongst the *Leucodendron*.

A WINTER'S TALE

An attractive winter's wreath in muted creams and golds makes a pleasant change from the usual seasonal reds and greens, and gives a different and stylish Christmas decoration. Begin by covering a wreath ring in moss, as shown in more detail on page 17.

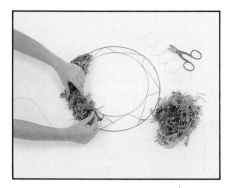

Wire together some clumps of cream sea lavender and virtually cover the entire ring with it. Next, take some purple statice and wire together several bunches.

Intersperse the purple statice evenly amongst the cream coloured flowers which form the base of the garland. Then, place at regular intervals some wired clumps of yarrow and rhodanthe (sunray).

Finally, gather about 10 to 12 cones and wire them together in a large bunch. With more wire fix the cones to the wreath at the front. Pull a few strands of the flowers between the cones to add contrast. Intersperse a few more cones throughout the wreath as shown to complete the picture. This combination of flowers and cones is remarkably inexpensive, yet the result is quite stunning.

This stunning wreath, with its wealth of contrasting colours and materials, makes a beautiful decoration to hang on the door at any time of the year. Begin by making a base (following the instructions given in full on page 17) using a wire frame and some moss. Cover the base with green wreath wrap.

Take some colourful fabric and cut it up into rectangles. Now wrap about 8 to 10 small foam spheres in the fabric, gathering the material at the top and securing with wire. Leave long wire 'tails' for attaching the balls to the frame. Position the spheres in groups of two or three at regular intervals around the wreath.

Wire clumps of green amaranthus (love-lies-bleeding) and insert them into the wreath, keeping them generally quite close to the fabric spheres.

Next, wire clumps of white larkspur and intersperse these amongst the amaranthus. These reflect the white in the fabric and add highlights to the arrangement. Wire together several groups of cones and place them standing upright in the arrangement so that they do not get lost among the other plants.

Soften the display by scattering bunches of soft pink rabbit's or hare's tail grass throughout. The seeds tend to moult very easily so be careful when wiring and inserting the grass not to overhandle it.

Pick out the colours in the fabric by dotting clumps of rust coloured nipplewort (or broom bloom) throughout. The dark tones will also add depth to the display.

Finish off with a few colourful satin bows. You can either make double bows (as described on page 15) or single ones as shown here. Insert the bows in amongst the fabric spheres, trailing the tails prettily over the arrangement.

SCOTTISH SALUTE

For the celebration of any Scottish event, such as Burns' night (January 26th), create this striking tartan wreath. First you will need to buy a twig ring from a florist. Begin the garland by individually wiring several heads of red rose. Arrange these in three small groups, evenly spaced around the ring.

Next, wire together nine small bunches of anaphalis (pearl everlasting) and push them into the ring so that they surround the roses. Take three lengths of tartan ribbon and make three single bows (following the instructions on page 15).

Take a fourth piece of ribbon, fold it in half and push a piece of wire through the folded end: this will form the long 'tails' of the arrangement. Cut a 'V' shape in the ends of the ribbons to finish them neatly, then wire a bow into each of the three gaps between the flowers. To complete the picture, wire the tartan tails beneath one of the bows.

HEARTS OF OAK

This unusual and imaginative wreath makes a striking decoration to hang on the door during the winter. To create it, you will first need to buy a twig wreath from your local florist. Begin the arrangement by wiring small bunches of oak leaves together. Also take a few pieces of sponge mushroom and push wires through one side.

Attach the leaves and fungus to the wreath, forming three groups evenly spaced around the ring. Now wire up some lotus seedheads — wiring the large ones singly and the small ones in groups of two or three. Insert these in amongst the other plants.

Push short lengths of wire as far as they will go through one end of some walnuts. Form small groups of about three to four nuts each by twisting the wires together. Slot the walnuts into the three groups of plants. Next add a few witch hazel twigs, allowing them to break out of the arrangement and cover some bare patches between the groups.

To finish, wire together several bunches of yarrow and slot them into the arrangement, using them to close up the gaps slightly between the three main groups. The yarrow adds necessary colour to the wreath and brings it to life.

Add style to the dinner table this Christmas with a striking centrepiece. Take a flat circular base — a cork mat or cake base will do — and glue single ruscus leaves around the edge. Stick three blocks of florists' foam on top, keep one taller than the others. Now insert the red candles into the foam, cutting them down as necessary to vary their heights.

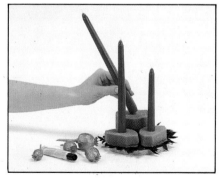

Build up the arrangement using gold-sprayed poppy heads, white helichrysum (strawflower or everlasting) and more ruscus leaves. The white adds essential highlights to the arrangement. Finish off by scattering single red roses throughout the display. The colours chosen here are especially for Christmas, but for other times of the year you can choose different colours.

This attractive 'woodland' design makes the perfect centrepiece for a stripped pine table. Begin by making a base out of three large dried leaves, such as these cobra leaves. Glue the leaves together, then glue a block of florists' foam on top. Wire up several cones and walnuts, forcing the wire through the base of the nuts as far as it will go.

Wire together clumps of oak leaves and build up the outline of the display. Now insert the nuts and cones, placing the former in small groups. Keep the shape irregular to make it more interesting. Brighten the display by scattering small clumps of ammobium (sandflower) throughout. To finish, trim a candle to the required length and push it firmly into the foam.

A pair of candlestick holders is transformed by a tightly-packed arrangement of dried flowers. For each stick, cut a sphere of florist's foam in half and hollow out the centre of each piece so that the foam sits snugly round the stem. Wrap a piece of florists' tape around the two halves to hold them together.

Push short stems of orange South African daisy (a form of helichrysum) into the foam, keeping the arrangement spherical. Then fill in with small wired clumps of red helichrysum (strawflower or everlasting) and pink miniature sunray, being sure not to leave any gaps.

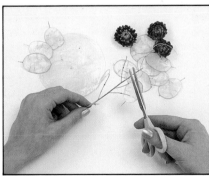

Create some pretty coasters using a few flowers and some mother-of-pearl discs. The latter can be bought from any shop specializing in shells. They should measure at least 4cm (1½in) more than the diameter of your glass base. Choose any combination of flowers or seedheads — shown above are helichrysum, honesty and hydrangea. Cut the heads off the plants.

Now create a ring around the edge of a shell by gluing the heads in position. The honesty can be stuck down first — the heads slightly overlapping — and the red helichrysum can be glued down on top at regular intervals. If you are only using helichrysum, alternate the colours for a more interesting effect.

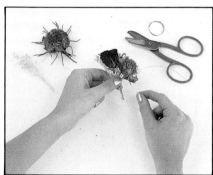

Dried flowers always enhance the dining table, especially when they are used so prettily to decorate the napkins. Buy a length of satin ribbon, choosing a colour to match (or, if you prefer, contrast) that of your napkins. Wire together a small bunch of flowers with silver wire; this posy contains bleached white nipplewort, a couple of long-eared pods and a single red rose.

Take about 35cm (14in) of ribbon per napkin and cut a V-shape in each end. Wrap ribbon round the stalk of the posy and tie a knot at the back, leaving one end longer than the other. Form a loop with the long end (for the napkin to go through) and tie a second knot. Bring the ends to the front of the posy and form a bow. The arrangement can now be put on the napkin.

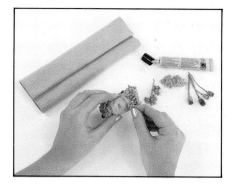

Try decorating some wooden napkin rings with a few dried flowers. You can either cover the ring entirely or make a pretty posy to tie on top. To do the former, simply cover the ring in glue. Then stick masses of tiny flowers on to it until the whole surface is covered. The flowers used here are yellow helichrysum, beige cluster-flowered sunray and poppy seedheads.

To make the posy gather a small square of pink spotted netting in the middle with a long piece of silver wire. Using the same wire, secure strands of beard grass on to the back of the netting, on either side as shown. Next add two pieces of coral, wiring them on in the same way. Finish off by arranging some South African daisies (helichrysum) and cluster-flowered sunray to the front.

Use plenty of fluffy cluster-flowered sunray to hide the wire. Finish off by tying the posy on to the ring with a length of white cord. In this way, by simply untying the cord, each of your supper guests can take home a small memento.

To make this splendid Christmas centrepiece, take a flat circular base such as a cake board and glue a cone of florists' foam to the centre. Then glue or staple a length of gold netting round the edge of the base, gathering it into bunches as you go. Crumple lengths of red fabric or ribbon into double loops and wire the ends. Arrange them in a ring on top of the gold.

Spray a number of Chinese lanterns and lotus seedheads with gold paint. When they are dry, wire the ends and insert them evenly spaced into the cone. Intersperse several long-eared pods throughout, pushing · them deep into the arrangement. Add highlights with a few honesty seedheads (silver dollar plant). Then wire together bunches of small red helichrysum (strawflower or everlasting) and dot them among the other plants, adding colour throughout. Finish off by inserting a few groups of white leaf skeletons — about two to three leaves per group.

FESTIVE MINIATURES

These miniature arrangements make pretty novelties to hang on the Christmas tree. One of them is made with cinnamon sticks. Take about three sticks and bind them together with wire. Wire on a double bow made out of gold gift wrap ribbon (following the instructions on page 15) and then add a posy of cones and small red helichrysum (strawflower or everlasting).

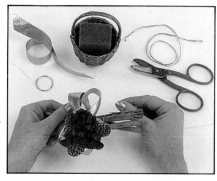

To make the other arrangement, first spray a small basket and some walnuts with gold paint. When these are dry, fill the basket with a block of florists' foam. Pack the foam with gold coloured South African daisies (a type of helichrysum) to form a spherical shape.

Push a length of wire through one end of each of the walnuts. Insert three or four nuts into the display, pushing them deep down amongst the flowers. Wire a small bow and attach it to the handle. Finally, hang each arrangement by means of a loop of gold cord.

Here are two more colourful decorations to hang on the Christmas tree. For the red ball, take a length of cord and wire the ends together, forming a loop. Push the wire right the way through a sphere of florists' foam and double it back on itself — into the foam — to secure. Now cover the foam with flowers.

Pack the flowers tightly into the foam to maintain the spherical shape. Those used here are deep red helichrysum (strawflower or everlasting). Fill in with little clumps of red nipplewort (or broom bloom). To finish, gather up and wire small pieces of silver netting, then insert them amongst the flowers.

For this design wire together a few flowers, such as these small white helichrysum and blue-dyed *Leucodendron brunia,* and attach three decorative bells. Gather up a piece of red netting and bind it on to the flowers. Make a double red bow as described on page 15, tie a long piece of ribbon round the middle (by which to hang the decoration) and attach the bow to the netting.

This beautiful design makes the perfect decoration for Valentine's day. Take some dry, bendy silver birch twigs, trim off all the rough ends and divide them into two equal bundles, about 60cm (24in) long. Join the two bundles at one end with stub wires, and again about 20cm (8in) further along. Now bend either side round to form a heart shape as shown.

Bind the three ends firmly with wire, then wrap wire around four other points on the heart to hold the twigs together. Cover each of the wired areas with red satin or gift wrap ribbon, gluing each strip in place at the back. Wire up a couple of red bows (as described on page 15) and put one on either side of the heart.

Attach a length of wired ribbon to the top of the heart for hanging. To soften the effect, take small clumps of gypsophilia (baby's breath) and push them in between the ribbon bands and the twigs. To finish off, mix some more gypsophilia with some tiny red spray roses and position them at the base of the heart.

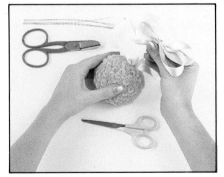

Hang this pretty pomander in the bedroom to add a splash of colour. First cut a length of ribbon and bind the ends together with a long piece of wire. Push the wire through a sphere of florists' foam to the far side, then double it back on itself to secure. Cut short stems of small yellow helichrysum (strawflower or everlasting) and cover the sphere with them.

Pack the flowers tightly into the ball, keeping them all at the same height to maintain the shape. Finally, make a double bow as described on page 15. Keep the tails very short so they do not show, then push the wires securing the bow into the foam, between the two strands of the loop.

Make your own ear-rings out of dried flowers and mother-of-pearl. The fittings can be bought in a craft shop or good department store, the mother-of-pearl from any shop specializing in shells. For each ear-ring, take two shell discs and pierce a hole through the top of each using a needle. Now thread the ear-ring pin through the holes, and bend it into a loop.

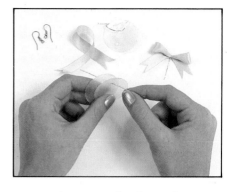

Using silver wire, bind together a small bunch of pink-dyed gypsophilia (baby's breath) and a couple of honesty seedheads (silver dollar plant). Make a small pink bow out of satin ribbon and wire it round the posy.

Glue the bunch on to the shells with an all-purpose adhesive. Alternatively, you can make a small hole at the bottom of the disc and wire the posy in position. Finally, attach the discs on to the ear-ring fitting using the looped pin.

Why not decorate your hair on a sunny day with this pretty hair slide? To begin, wire the plants individually; shown here are small pink helichrysum (strawflower or everlasting), South African daisies (also helichrysum), moon grass, leaf skeletons and small cones. Then tie them into a bunch by gradually binding them together with a single piece of silver wire.

To finish simply glue the bunch on to a plastic hair slide using an all-purpose adhesive.

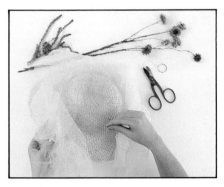

Cut a dash in this stunning and original design made simply from a plain straw hat and just two varieties of flower. First cut a length of pink netting, long enough to wind around the crown of the hat and leave a modest train. Gather the net loosely round the hat and either stitch or wire the fabric to the front and back of the crown.

Using silver wire, tie together a bunch of acroclinium (sunray) and long stems of rat's tail statice. Attach the flowers to the back of the hat, winding the wire securely around the netting. To finish, make a double bow with long trailing tails out of pink satin ribbon — following instructions on page 15. Attach the bow to the hat, using it to cover up any wire that still shows.

ALL AROUND MY HAT

A small straw hat, decorated with a garland of dried flowers, makes a pretty design to hang on the bedroom wall. This particular hat is a small doll's hat. Begin by making three bows out of satin ribbon, as described on page 15. Tie a second length of ribbon round the middle of one of the bows to form the long 'tails' at the back of the hat.

Make a garland to wrap around the crown as follows. Attach some rose wire to a length of string, about 20-25cm (8-10in) from one end. Place a small bunch of flowers over the join and secure with the wire. Add another bunch to cover the stems of the first and bind as before. Continue adding to the garland in this way until it is the desired length.

The flowers used in this garland are red amaranthus (love-lies-bleeding), South African daisy (helichrysum) and golden dryandra. Wrap the garland round the crown and tie the ends of the string together to secure. Wire a couple of bows to the front of the hat and put the other one over the join at the back.

A delicate posy of dried flowers provides a perfect decoration for any gift. Choose a selection of brightly coloured, small-headed flowers and tie them together with fine wire. The flowers used here are blue larkspur, yellow South African daisy, (a type of helichrysum), small red roses and a touch of golden rod. Wrap a strip of white ribbon around the stems and finish off with a bow.

The posy on this gift box is made up in a similar way, using flowers in a range of colours that match those of the box. The posy contains green amaranthus (love-lies-bleeding), mauve xeranthemums, pink gypsophilia (baby's breath), blue larkspur, cream 'cauliflower' and yellow dudinea.

Attach the posies to the gifts with glue. Alternatively you can wire them on. To do this you will need to pierce two small holes in the side of the box. Wrap wire round the stems of the posy and thread it through the holes; secure on the inside.

This pretty miniature display, arranged in a tiny gift box, would make a delightful present. And with all that lavender, it smells as lovely as it looks. First cut a small block of florists' foam and pop it inside the box. Then wire a couple of red ribbons.

Wire together bunches of lavender and pack them into the foam, keeping the arrangement tallest in the middle and splaying it out at the sides. Now scatter tiny, daisy-like glixia or grass daisies throughout; push some deep into the display. Finish off by attaching the two red bows, one to the box, the other higher up on a stem of lavender.

The perfect Easter present — an attractive egg-shaped gift box filled with a mass of pretty flowers. The flowers have been specially chosen to reflect the colours of the box, creating a very co-ordinated effect. Cut a section from a sphere of florists' foam and put it in the base. Secure it with tape. Place the lid about a third of the way across the foam and again tape in place.

Build up the outline using brown grass and green amaranthus (love-lies-bleeding). Use some of the amaranthus leaves to add contrast of texture. Intersperse the display with a few small bunches of tiny red helichrysum, placing them well into the arrangement to give depth.

To finish, dot a number of South African daisies (a form of helichrysum) throughout the arrangement. Provided the stems are strong, these can be added singly without wiring.

In this attractive arrangement, peachy coloured flowers set off a small brass trinket box to perfection. Cut a section from a cylinder of florists' foam to fit inside the box and secure with a strip of florists' tape.

Build up the shape of the display with cluster-flowered sunray and a few strands of creamy nipplewort (or broom bloom). The latter will add a fluffy softness to the arrangement.

Next add the focal flowers which are peachy South African daisies (a type of helichrysum). Wire them in small groups and intersperse them throughout. Finish off with a few cones to add an interesting contrast of colour and texture.

This little collection of hanging baskets would be a pretty addition to a bedroom or bathroom. Take three small straw baskets and place a piece of dry florists' foam inside each one. Take several clumps of wired pink miniature sunray and insert them in the first basket, keeping the flowers close to the foam so that they almost cover it.

Among the sunray place small pieces of *Leucodendron brunia* to give a contrasting texture. These, along with the sunray, should virtually fill the basket.

Next, bunch together some fluffy heads of rabbit's or hare's tail grass. Keep them taller than the other flowers so that, when slotted in, they rise above the outline.

Finally, make some little bows from pink satin ribbon (following the instructions on page 15) and place one bow on each side of the basket. All three baskets are completed in exactly the same way.

Once the three baskets are finished, tie a piece of co-ordinating cord to each basket handle. Tie all the cords together at the top so that the baskets hang one beneath the other and complete with another pink satin bow.

POT-POURRI BASKETS

These attractive baskets filled with pot-pourri will look very pretty hanging from the dressing table, adding colour and fragrance to your bedroom. Choose a couple of miniature baskets with narrow handles. Head some pink acroclinium (sunray) and glue them round the rim of the baskets. Position them in an uneven ring to make room for the other flowers.

Fill in with heads of larkspur and purple statice, alternating the colours. Glue some of the flower heads half way up the handle on either side.

When the rim is completely covered and the glue dry, make a double bow out of narrow pink ribbon (following the instructions on page 15) and wire it to the top of the handle. Tie a second length of wider, contrasting ribbon around the centre of the bow, leaving long tails for hanging the basket. Finally, fill the basket with pot-pourri.

FLORAL MOBILE

Use some foam spheres, flowers and fabric to make this pretty mobile. Take five spheres of florists' foam. Then cut five circles of fabric, large enough to cover the balls and allowing extra to be gathered up. Experiment with a piece of paper first to determine the correct size of the circle. Wrap each piece of fabric around a ball and secure at the top with silver wire.

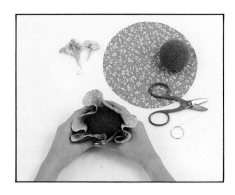

Make five small posies from pale blue helichrysum and nipplewort (or broom bloom). Tie the posies with silver wire, leaving a short tail which can then be pushed into the neck of the sphere. Next, cut five lengths of thin cord or ribbon and wind around the top of each ball. Tie a piece of matching ribbon around the neck of the balls and finish with a bow.

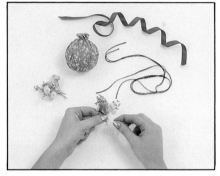

Wire more of the same flowers into bunches and stick them into a small piece of florists' foam to form a ball of flowers. Tie two pieces of dowling together at the centre with thin cord; leave two long tails of cord for hanging the mobile. Hang four bundles from the arms of the mobile, the fifth from the centre. Attach the floral 'pomander' by a longer cord from the centre.

These tiny pot-pourri bags are so easy to create, and they make delightful gifts. Take a length of cotton fabric and, using a plate as a pattern, cut out a circle about 25-30cm (10-12in) in diameter. Hem the edge with running stitch, leaving long tails of thread at either end. Cup the fabric circle in your hand as shown and fill it with pot-pourri.

Gather the fabric into a tight ball by pulling the threads. Secure with a knot. Wire together a small tight bunch of helichrysum (strawflower or everlasting) using fine silver rose wire and attach the posy to the bag, threading the wire through the fabric on both sides to secure. (Use a needle to make holes in the fabric first if necessary.)

Make a double bow out of satin ribbon (following the instructions on page 15,) and wire this on to the bag. Finally, cut a length of gold cord about 35cm (15in) long and tie it round the posy, finishing with a double knot. Tie the ends of the cords at the desired length and hang the bag by this loop.

This fragrant string of pot-pourri bags, designed to hang in the bedroom, makes a delightful gift. First take a square of fabric and, craddling it in the palm of your hand, fill the centre with pot-pourri. Then gather the edges together, turning them in as you do so to make a wide 'hem'. Secure the fabric with wire, making a small ball. Repeat two or more times.

For each bag, make a double bow out of two lengths of wide satin ribbon, tying the second bow round the centre of the first. Gather a few delicate flowers into a small bouquet and wire the stems firmly together. Shown here are deep pink rabbit's or hare's tail grass, some large — and small — flowered helichrysum (strawflower or everlasting) and blue nipplewort (or broom bloom).

Wire the bunch around the neck of a pot-pourri bag and attach the bow, either with wire or a short length of ribbon. Repeat for the other bags. Finally, take a length of cord and tie the balls together at regular intervals.

Three clam shells provide the perfect setting for a colourful miniature arrangement. First you must carefully bore a hole in the base of each shell using a braddle. Now fix the shells together with wire, fanning two of them out as shown and using the third as a base. Slice a section off a sphere of florists' foam and cut it to fit the base of the shells. Glue the foam in position.

Cut off a number of honesty (silver dollar plant) seedheads and insert them singly into the foam, covering it completely. Next add small wired bunches of tiny red roses, concentrating them in the middle. Follow with clumps of golden quaking grass, positioning them so that they fan out from the centre of the arrangement and form a star-shaped outline.

Fill in amongst the quaking grass with clumps of bright yellow cluster-flowered helichrysum (strawflower or everlasting), packing them tightly into the arrangement.

Once again clams have been used as the setting for a display, this time in conjunction with a 'fan' of coral to follow through the marine theme. Carefully bore a hole in the base of each shell using a braddle and fix the shells together in an open position with wire. Tape a block of florists' foam into the base and begin to build up the fan with pieces of rust coloured coral.

Now fill in using wired clumps of cluster-flowered sunray and cream anaphalis, keeping them much shorter than the coral and covering most of the foam. Allow fluffy strands of sunray to spill over the rim of the base shell.

Insert two or three long-eared pods deep into the arrangement to add depth and interest. Finally add the focal flowers by positioning tight groups of South African daisies (a form of helichrysum). Peachy coloured ones have been chosen here to blend with the soft tones of the coral.

A clam shell makes an ideal setting for this pretty miniature arrangement. Cut a small block of florists' foam and place it in the bottom of one of the shell halves, securing it with florists' fixative or glue. Position a second shell on top and glue the two shells firmly together as shown.

Wire small clumps of pink gypsophilia (baby's breath) and red nipplewort (or broom bloom). Pack them into the florists' foam, forming the outline of the arrangement. Allow a few strands of gypsophilia to trail over the edge of the shell.

Add several wired strands of blue-dyed *Leucodendron brunia* to provide a strong contrast in colour, and finish off with two or three pieces of red amaranthus (love-lies-bleeding).

The colours of this small conch have been cleverly picked out in the soft pinks and creams of the delicate arrangement. First cut a small block of florists' foam and wedge it into the neck of the shell. Then wire up a few seedheads of honesty (silver dollar plant) and position them in the foam.

Next insert several large heads of soft pink helichrysum (strawflower or everlasting). Fill in any gaps with bunches of small white helichrysum.

Finally, wire together small bunches of pink rabbit's or hare's tails grass and intersperse them among the arrangement so that they stand up above the other flowers, softly breaking through the outline.

A combination of lemon yellow flowers and turquoise netting creates a bright, fresh look that will add a touch of spring even in mid winter! The plants used are yellow helichrysum, cluster-flowered sunray and bleached white rabbit's or hare's tail grass. Bind a few plants together with silver reel wire and continue to add flowers, gradually building up a dome-shaped posy.

Keep the rabbit's tail grass taller than the other flowers to break through the outline of the dome. When the shape has been formed, finish off the binding and trim the ends. Wire together long loops of lemon and pale green ribbon and attach them to the posy.

Take a large square of netting and place the posy in the centre. Fold the edges of the netting under and gather the material around the stem of the posy, securing it firmly with wire. Finish off by attaching a lemon bow to the 'handle' of the bouquet.

This attractive miniature arrangement will fill your bedroom with the sweet smell of lavender. Slice a sphere of florists' foam in half, then cut out a circle of fabric, large enough to wrap around one of the pieces with plenty to spare. Hem the circle, then wrap it round the foam piece.

Secure the fabric with a strip of ribbon tied in a bow. Make sure you leave some foam exposed at the top so that you can pack it with lavender. Wire the lavender into bunches and fill the bag with it. Then insert some soft pink rabbit's or hare's tail grass. Finish off with a couple of wired strands of ribbon draped over the display.

With its soft muted tones and shiny satin ribbons this pretty swag will add a touch of romance to your bedroom. To make it you will need a length of muslin, some satin ribbon and a selection of plants. Used here are pink rhodanthe (sunray), pink wheat, oak leaves and leaf skeletons. Begin by wiring the plants individually into large clumps, leaving long 'tails' of wire.

Cut a strip of muslin about 15cm (6in) wide and 100cm (40in) long. Beginning at one end, gather some of the material into a bunch and secure it by wiring on a bunch of rhodanthe. Repeat the process at regular intervals along the length of the fabric, gathering the muslin into soft folds each time.

To add contrast and depth to the arrangement add clumps of rusty brown oak leaves and whispy leaf skeletons to the rhodanthe. Then attach the pink wheat, arranging it amongst the folds of material.

Make up several double bows using the method described on page 15 and wire them on to the groups of flowers. Use the bows to conceal any wire still showing. Add a couple of long trailing strands of ribbon for the finishing touch. Drape the swag across the end of your bed or around a large mirror.

A n attractive wall hanging arrangement puts a redundant towel ring to good use. Begin by slicing a sphere of florists' foam in half and cutting away the centre of one piece so that it fits snugly on top of the ring. Secure the foam with a couple of strips of florists' tape.

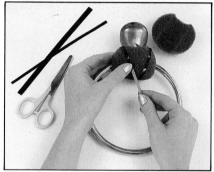

Form the outline of the arrangement with 'blue leaf' foliage. Balance the general shape with that of the ring but create a spiky effect. Fill in with three or so long-eared pods, packed tightly into the foam, and several clumps of beige cluster-flowered sunray. Concentrate the latter in the centre of the arrangement.

Finish off with large bold clumps of yellow helichrysum (strawflower or everlasting) to brighten up the arrangement and blend with the rich tones of the brass ring.

PINK POT-POURRI

Create a pretty design for the bathroom using an ornamental shaving mug. First cut a small circle of wire mesh, crumple it into a ball and pack it into the spout of the mug.

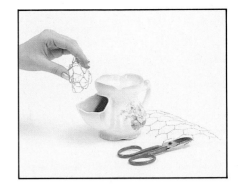

Pack the mesh with clumps of miniature sunray so that they appear to be spilling over the sides of the spout. Then fill in the gaps with wired clumps of *Helichrysum casianum*. Add interesting textures with groups of bobbly pink-dyed *Leucodendron brunia*.

Soften the arrangement by scattering a few fluffy pink feathers throughout. To finish, fill the top of the jug with fragrant pot-pourri.

SCIENTIFIC CLASSIFICATION

The following is an alphabetical list of the common names of plants used in this book and their Latin equivalents

Common name	Latin name	Common name	Latin name
Acroclinium (Sunray)	Acroclinium roseum = Helipterum roseum	Nipplewort (Dutch exporters call it broom bloom)	Laspana communis
Baby's breath	Gypsophilia paniculata		
Barley, black-eared	Hordeum	Oats, wild	Avena fatua
Beard grass	Polypogon	Pearl everlasting	Anaphalis
Bells of Ireland	Moluccella laevis	Poppy	Papaver
Bottlebrush	Callistemon	Quaking grass	Briza maxima
Celosia	Celosia argentea plumosa	Rhodanthe (Sunray)	Rhodanthe manglesii = Helipterum manglesii
Chinese lantern	Physalis alkekengi frangetii		
Clubrush	Scirpus	Rabbit's or hare's tail grass	Lagarus ovatus
Glixia (grass daisy)	Aphyllanthes monspeliensis		
Globe thistle	Echinops	Rat's tail statice	Limonium suworowii
Golden rod	Solidago	Reed	Phragmites australis
Honesty (silver dollar plant)	Lunaria annua	Reed grass	Phalaris arundinacea
		Rose	Rosa
Lady's mantle	Alchemilla mollis	Sandflower	Ammobium alatum
Lamb's tongue	Stachys lanata	Safflower	Carthamus tinctorius
Larkspur	Delphinium consolida	Sea holly	Eryngium oliverianum
Lavender	Lavandula angustifolia (often sold as L. spica or L. officinalis)	Sea lavender	Limonium tataricum
		Statice	Limonium sinuatum
		Strawflower (or everlasting)	Helichrysum
Lotus flower	Nelumbo lutea		
Love-in-a-mist	Nigella damascena	Sunray	Helipterum
Love-lies-bleeding	Amaranthus caudatus	Yarrow	Achillea

DRYING METHODS

Suitable Plants for Air Drying

Acanthus	Eucalyptus leaves	Iris seedheads	Protea
Acroclinium	Gladioli seedheads	Lady's mantle	Rhodanthe
Anaphalis	Globe thistle seedheads	Larkspur	Rose
Bamboo	Golden rod	Lavender	Sea holly
Barley	Grasses	Lotus seedheads	Sea lavender
Bells of Ireland	Gypsophilia	Love-in-a-mist	Shepherd's purse
Bottlebrush	Heather	Lupin seedheads	Statice
Chinese lantern	Helichrysum	Mimosa	Sunray
Clary	Hogweed seedheads	Monkshood	Sweetcorn
Cornflower	Hollyhock seedheads	Moss	Teasel seedheads
Cow parsley seedheads	Honesty seedheads	Oats	Thistle seedheads
Delphinium	Hops	Onion seedheads	Wheat
Dock	Hydrangea	Poppy seedheads	Xeranthemum

Suitable Plants for Preserving in Desiccants

Anemone	Delphinium	Hollyhock	Orchid
Buttercup	Elder	Larkspur	Paeony
Camellia	Forget-me-not	Lily flowerheads	Pansy
Cornflower	Freesia	Marigold	Primrose
Daffodil	Gentian	Mimosa	Ranunculus
Dahlia	Geranium	Bells of Ireland	Rose
Daisy	Hellibore	Monkshood	Violet

Suitable Plants for Preserving in Glycerine

Aspidistra leaves	Chestnut leaves	Ivy leaves	Oats
Barley	Eucalyptus leaves	Lady's mantle	Old man's beard
Beech leaves	Hawthorn leaves	Laurel leaves	Quaking grass
Bells of Ireland	Holly leaves	Magnolia leaves	Rabbit's or hare's tail grass
Box leaves	Hops	Mahonia leaves	
Bracken	Hydrangea	Oak leaves	Wheat